Rockets

Wendy Hinote Lanier

AV2
www.av2books.com

Step 1
Go to **www.av2books.com**

Step 2
Enter this unique code

BPWMGMFJ4

Step 3
Explore your interactive eBook!

AV2 is optimized for use on any device

Your interactive eBook comes with...

Contents
Browse a live contents page to easily navigate through resources

Audio
Listen to sections of the book read aloud

Videos
Watch informative video clips

Weblinks
Gain additional information for research

Try This!
Complete activities and hands-on experiments

Key Words
Study vocabulary, and complete a matching word activity

Quizzes
Test your knowledge

Slideshows
View images and captions

... and much, much more!

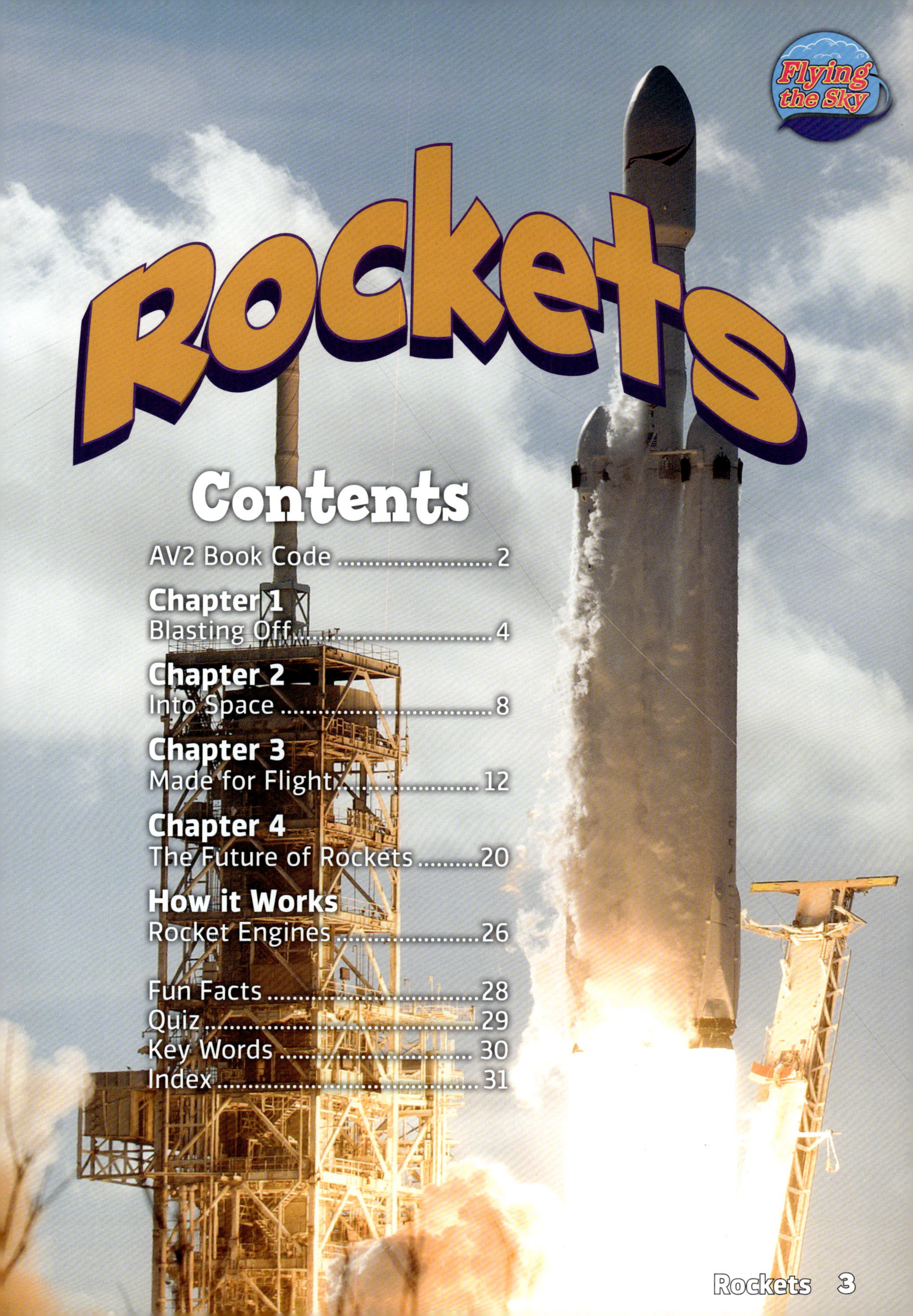

Rockets

Contents

Chapter 1

Blasting Off

The Falcon Heavy rocket travels into space.

A giant rocket sits on the launch pad. It is about to blast off. The rocket is 23 stories tall. It is built to carry heavy **cargo**. The rocket is called the Falcon Heavy. Today, it will make its first trip to space.

The rocket's engines roar to life. They shoot out hot gases. The rocket zooms up into the air.

A Falcon Heavy rocket launches at the Kennedy Space Center in Florida.

Pieces of the rocket come apart as it flies. First, the two rocket **boosters** use up their fuel. They fall away from the main rocket.

Soon after, the main rocket releases the upper **stage**. The rocket returns to the ground, but the upper stage keeps flying through space. It will travel around the Sun.

After falling off the main rocket, the Falcon Heavy boosters fly back to the launch pad.

Chapter 2

Into Space

Robert Goddard designed several early rockets. He wanted to send rockets to the Moon.

Germany developed V-2 rockets during World War II (1939–1945).

The first rockets were fireworks. They were invented hundreds of years ago in China. Robert Goddard built the first modern rocket in 1926. It used oxygen and gasoline to produce power.

Rockets first reached space in the 1940s. At this time, Germany began building rocket **missiles**. The Soviet Union and the United States studied these rockets. They tried to build their own. The Soviet Union sent a rocket to space in 1957. The rocket released a **satellite**. This was the first object a rocket sent to space.

Another Soviet rocket carried a man to space in 1961. He became the first person to orbit Earth. The next year, the United States sent a person into orbit.

By the 2000s, rockets had many uses. They carried satellites and spacecraft. Rockets launched space shuttles, too. The shuttles carried **astronauts** and supplies to the International Space Station (ISS).

Race to the Moon

In the 1960s, the United States wanted to send a person to the Moon. So did the Soviet Union. Each country wanted to be first. A U.S. spacecraft landed on the Moon in 1969. Saturn V rockets launched the U.S. spacecraft.

Chapter 3

Made for Flight

The nose cone is attached to the top of the rocket.

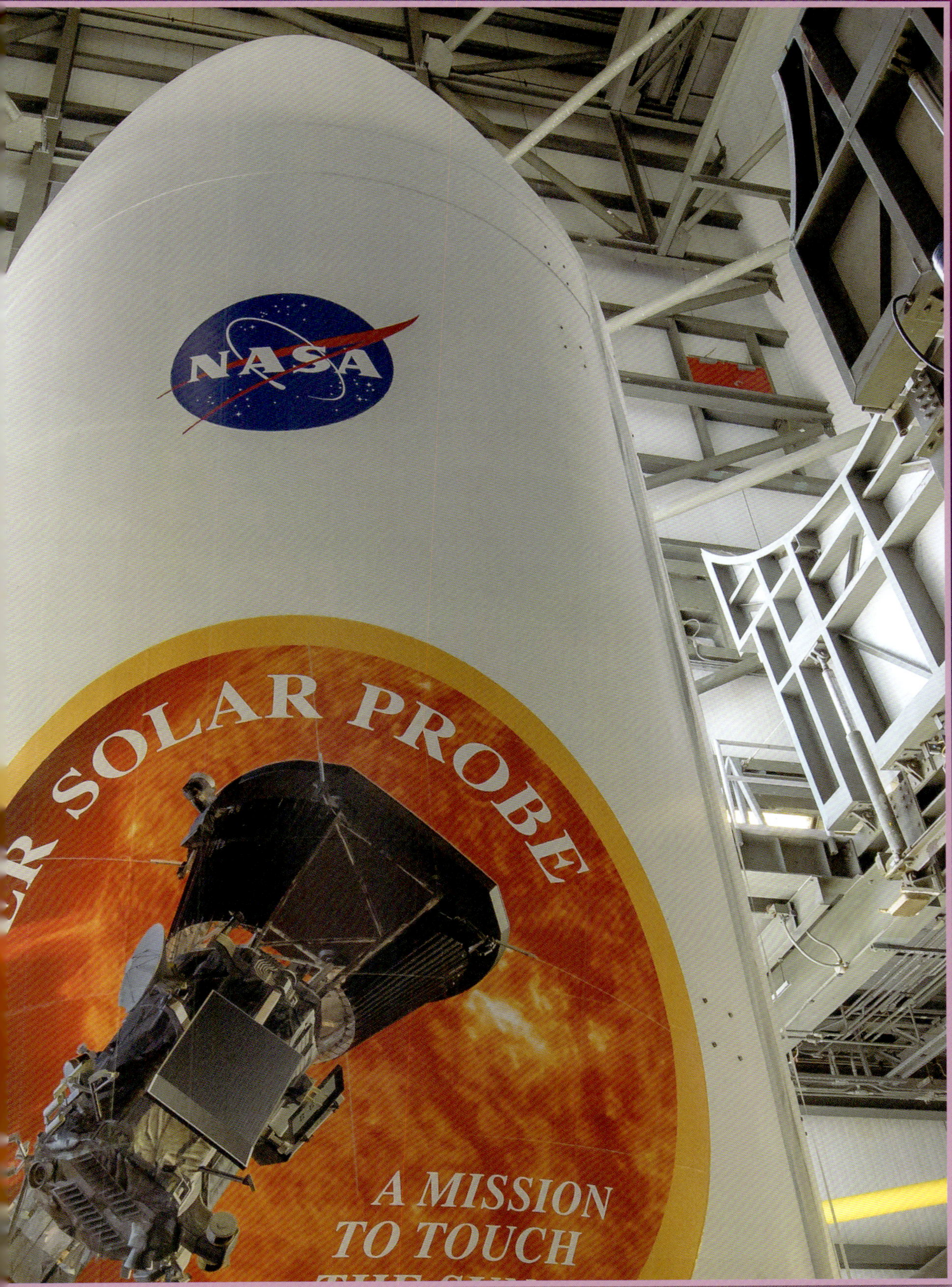
NASA
SOLAR PROBE
A MISSION
TO TOUCH

Rockets carry people and cargo to space. A rocket's cargo is also called its payload. The payload goes inside the rocket's nose cone. This part protects the payload until it reaches space.

Zenit rockets have carried several satellites to space.

To reach space, rockets must escape the pull of Earth's **gravity**. They need lots of energy to do this, and they must go very fast. So, rockets have powerful engines.

In fact, the biggest part of a rocket is the **propulsion** system. This system includes the main rocket and the rocket boosters. Most boosters burn solid fuel. After they use up the fuel, the boosters fall off the rocket. That way, their weight does not slow the rocket as it travels.

Rocket Speed

Rockets reach very high speeds. They can go 25,000 miles per hour (40,000 kilometers per hour). That is 7 miles (11 km) every second. A rocket can travel to space in three minutes. If a car could drive to space, it would take 60 minutes.

A guidance system controls the rocket's flight. This system has many parts. It uses sensors, computers, and **radars**. All these parts work together. They steer the rocket. They also keep the rocket steady as it flies.

The cockpit of the *Atlantis* Space Shuttle was designed to provide astronauts with all the information they needed during flight.

Parts of a Rocket

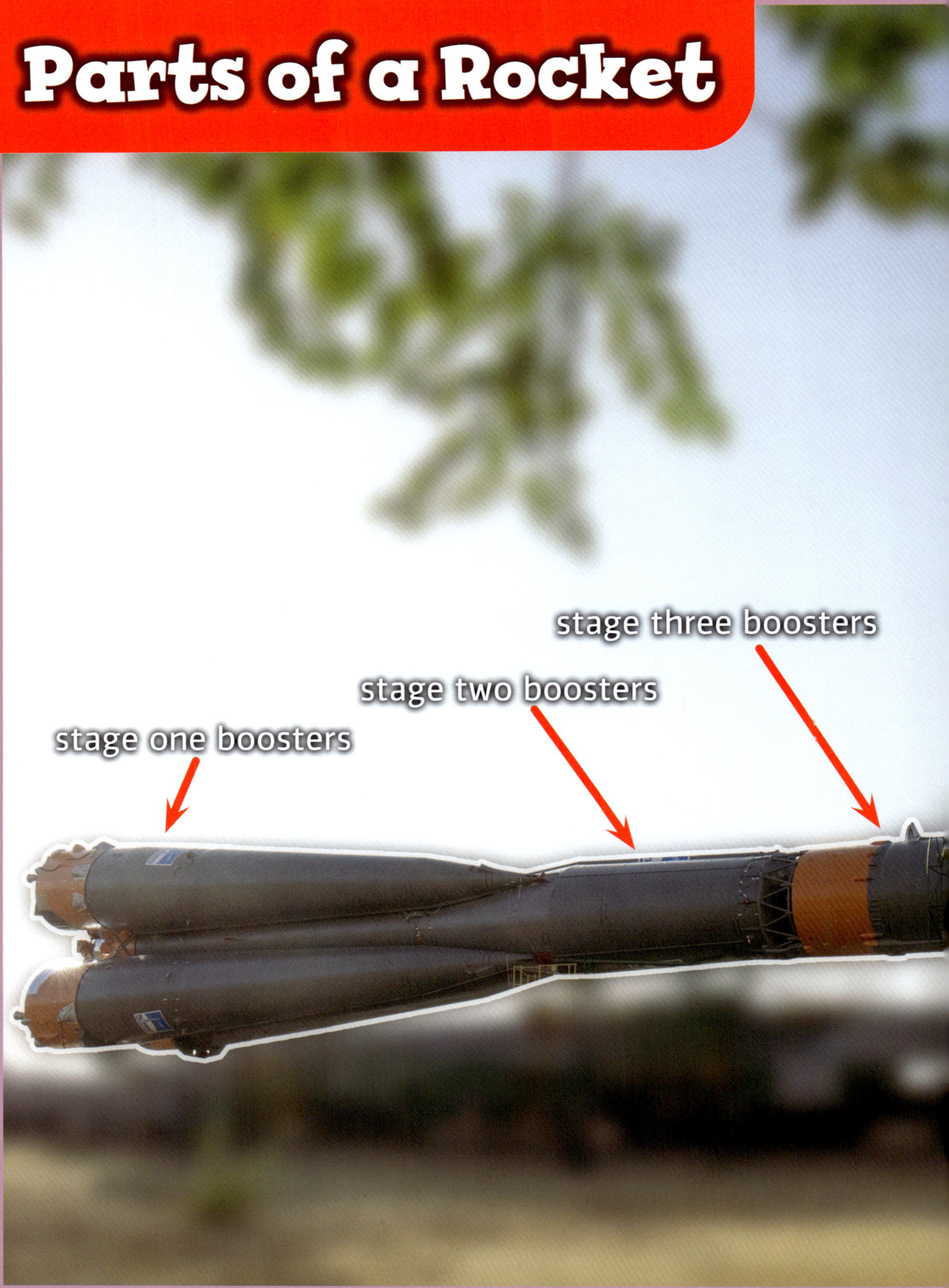

main rocket
nose cone

Chapter 4

The Future of Rockets

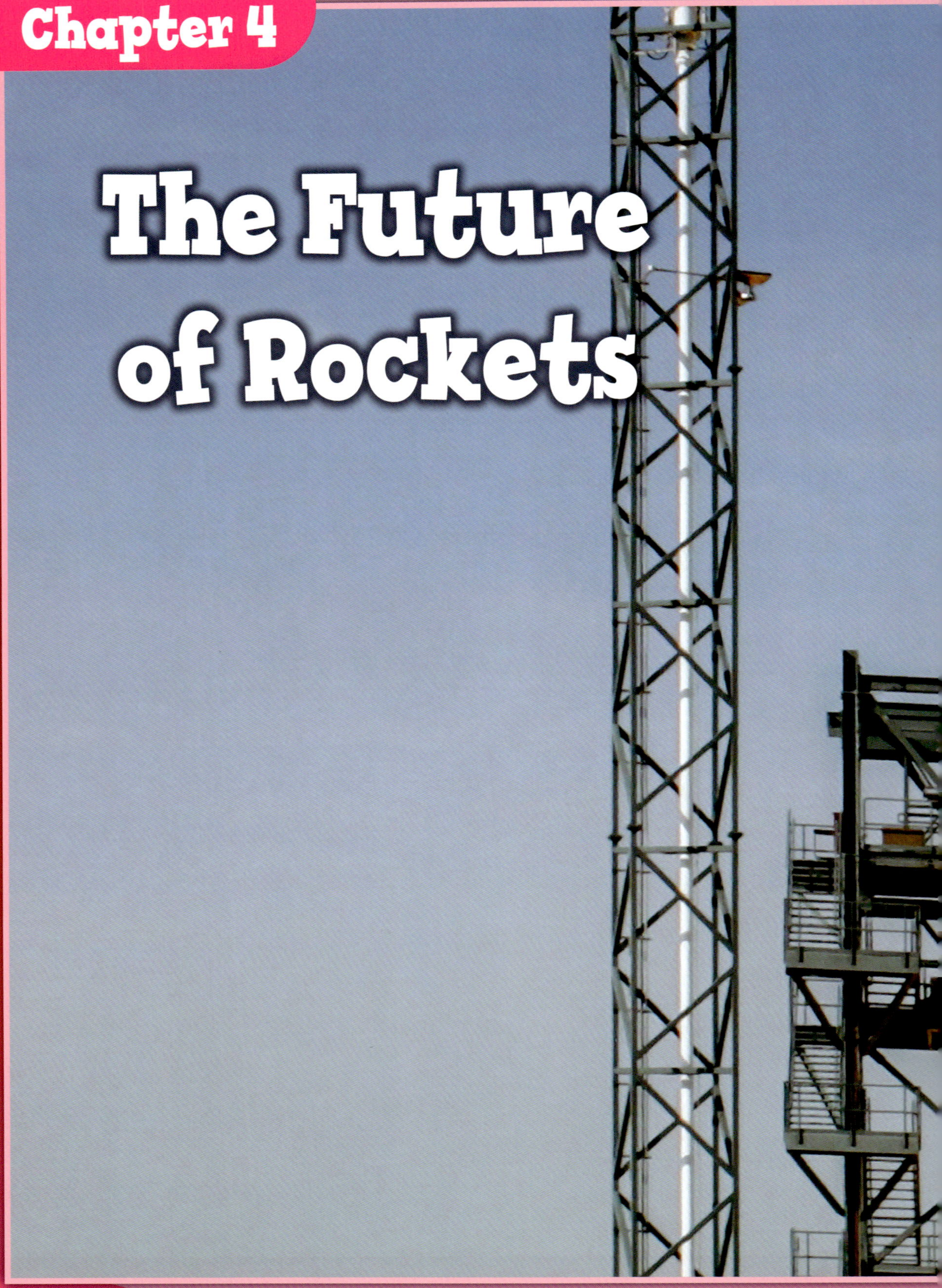

Blue Origin is one company that has launched and landed a reusable rocket.

Rockets are very expensive. For many years, only governments could afford to build them. That is beginning to change. A few private companies have started making rockets.

The first one was SpaceX. This company launched its first rocket in 2010. Since then, several other companies have launched rockets. They include Virgin Galactic and Blue Origin. Each company has its own design.

Vacation in Space

A few companies are designing rockets that will carry tourists. The rockets will take people on a short trip to space. The companies hope to make space travel more common. People will buy tickets to ride inside the rockets. They may even be able to visit the ISS.

The Skybolt 2 rocket is designed by a British company called Starchaser Industries.

In most older rockets, the engines and boosters were used only once. Then, these parts dropped off the rocket. They burned up as they fell back to Earth. Many newer rockets have reusable parts. These parts can be used over and over.

The Space Shuttle External Fuel tank would detach from the space shuttle about nine minutes into a flight.

Scientists on the ground help find and steer the parts of the rocket that fall back to Earth.

Some parts fall into the ocean. Boats pick them up. They bring the parts back to land to use again. Other parts fly back to the launch pad. They land there. Then, they are used for other rockets. Using parts again is less expensive. In time, sending rockets to space may not cost as much.

How it Works

Rocket Engines

Engines burn fuel to produce power. An engine needs oxygen to burn fuel. However, there is no oxygen in space.

To solve this problem, rockets carry oxygen. Pumps send the oxygen and fuel to the combustion chamber. In this space, the oxygen and fuel mix together. The mixture is then burned to make a blast of hot gases. The gases shoot the rocket up off the ground. The rocket flies into the air. Then, the gases shoot out the back of the rocket. They cause the rocket to move forward.

Nozzles at the bottom of a rocket shoot out hot gases.

Fun Facts

The Falcon Heavy carried an electric car to space. A dummy named Starman rode in the car.

A rocket launched the Juno spacecraft in 2011. The spacecraft reached Jupiter five years later.

A spaceship launched by a SpaceX rocket first reached the ISS in 2012.

The Falcon Heavy has 27 engines. Together, they create as much power as 18 airplanes.

Quiz

1 In what year did SpaceX launch its first rocket?

2 What is another name for a rocket's cargo?

3 What does an engine need in order to burn fuel?

4 What were the first rockets?

5 How long does it take a rocket to travel to space?

6 Who built the first modern rocket?

Answers: 1. 2010 **2.** Payload **3.** Oxygen **4.** Fireworks **5.** Three minutes **6.** Robert Goddard

Key Words

astronauts: people who are trained to work or travel in space

boosters: small rockets added to the side of a large rocket to provide extra power

cargo: items carried by a vehicle from one place to another

gravity: the natural force that pulls objects toward Earth

missiles: weapons that are fired or launched at a target

propulsion: used for moving a vehicle forward

radars: devices that send out radio waves for detecting and locating objects

satellite: an object or vehicle that orbits a planet or moon, often to collect information

stage: one of the several sections that make up a rocket. Each stage has its own fuel and engine. Only the upper stage carries the payload.

Index

Get the best of both worlds.

AV2 bridges the gap between print and digital.

The expandable resources toolbar enables quick access to content including **videos**, **audio**, **activities**, **weblinks**, **slideshows**, **quizzes**, and **key words**.

Animated videos make static images come alive.

Resource icons on each page help readers to further **explore key concepts**.

Published by AV2
350 5th Avenue, 59th Floor
New York, NY 10118
Website: www.av2books.com

Library of Congress Control Number: 2019953852

ISBN 978-1-7911-1872-3 (hardcover)
ISBN 978-1-7911-1873-0 (softcover)
ISBN 978-1-7911-1874-7 (multi-user eBook)
ISBN 978-1-7911-1875-4 (single user eBook)

Printed in Guangzhou, China
1 2 3 4 5 6 7 8 9 0 24 23 22 21 20

032020
101319

Project Coordinator: Ryan Smith Designer: Sushant Deshpande

Every reasonable effort has been made to trace ownership and to obtain permission to reprint copyright material. The publishers would be pleased to have any errors or omissions brought to their attention so that they may be corrected in subsequent printings.

AV2 acknowledges Getty Images, iStock, Shutterstock, and Alamy as its primary image suppliers for this title.

First published by North Star Editions in 2019.